home
SWEET HOME

THIS COLORING BOOK

belongs to

____
____

Stay
home

STAY HAPPY STAY HOME

STAY
HOME
SAVE
LIVES

e-book

Stay Home
and
READ
E-books

STAY
6FT
AWAY

STAY
STRONG

WASH
YOUR
hands
STAY HOME

NEVER LOSE
HOPE

HAVE
faith
in
LORd

Stay
home
Save
lives

Use a
HAND
SANITISER

always
wear a
mask

STAY AT
HOME AND
STAY
HEALTHY

STAY AT
HOME
AND
STAY
HAPPY
!!!!!!

Stay at Home.
Better Safe than
Sorry.

Stay at Home

stay home . stay safe
stay
sane
and read books

home
SWEET HOME

LETS STAY

SAFE

just

stay

home

stay

HOME

stay
home
stay
safe

stay home
stay safe
stay lives

stay home
stay safe

www.ingramcontent.com/pod-product-compliance
Lightning Source LLC
Chambersburg PA
CBHW081830250726
48657CB00011B/3547